BLACK BART SAYS DRAW

ISBN: 0-8362-1869-8

Library of Congress Catalog Card Number: 90-85467

Black Bart Says Draw

A Fox Trot Collection
by Bill Amend

Andrews and McMeel
A Universal Press Syndicate Company
Kansas City

To
Kristin

JASON, WILL YOU QUIT ROAMING AROUND THE HOUSE?!

LONE IGUANA BREAKING IN NEW HORSE, SILVER JUNIOR.

GIMME THAT!

HEY!

AMEND

AAAAA! SILVER JUNIOR!

SNAP!

THERE— HE'S BROKEN.

NO NO— SHOOT THE HORSE FIRST, KEMOSABE.

KISSIN' LIPS   ELLE

NOW WHAT?

LONE IGUANA WANT YOU TO HAVE SILVER BULLET.

ssin' Lin-   ELLE

FWAP!

AMEND

MOTH-ERRR!

LONE IGUANA WANT YOU TO HAVE ANOTHER SILVER BULLET...

WHAT HAPPENED TO THE LONE IGUANA?

BLACK BART KILLED HIM IN A GUNFIGHT.

CAN'T SAY I'M SORRY.

CAN'T SAY I'M THRILLED EITHER.

BLACK BART SAYS "DRAW."

FoxTrot
by Bill Amend

WAIT A MINUTE...
THIS SHIRT—
IT SMELLS LIKE...
LIKE...

PAIGE!...

ALL RIGHT, PAIGE, THIS IS IT— YOU'RE DEAD! I TOLD YOU TO **STOP** WEARING MY CLOTHES!

WHAT ARE YOU TALKING ABOUT?! I HAVEN'T WORN YOUR CLOTHES IN MONTHS!

OH YEAH? YOU WANT TO EXPLAIN WHY MY JEAN JACKET SMELLS LIKE GIORGIO PERFUME?!

BEATS ME.

OR WHY MY RED SWEATER SMELLS LIKE COCO? OR WHY MY PINK SHIRT SMELLS LIKE OPIUM? OR WHY MY BLUE T-SHIRT SMELLS LIKE LIZ CLAIBORNE?

PETER, WILL YOU CALM DOWN?!

OR WHY MY SCARF SMELLS LIKE OBSESSION? OR WHY MY SWEATS SMELL LIKE LAUREN? OR WHY MY GREEN WINDBREAKER SMELLS LIKE COLORS?

AMEND

OR WHY MY FAVORITE SWEATSHIRT SMELLS LIKE... LIKE...

WHITE LINEN?

WHAT? IT WAS JUST A LUCKY GUESS. REALLY. HONEST. CRUD.

DENISE, NOW I KNOW YOU'RE MATURE ENOUGH TO HANDLE THIS...

HANDLE WHAT?

I THINK MAYBE, POSSIBLY, SORT OF... WE SHOULD DATE OTHER PEOPLE.

WHAT?!

I JUST THINK IT'S BEST...

LET'S HOPE I'M MATURE ENOUGH TO HANDLE THIS.

IS IT SOMETHING I DID?...

DENISE, WE'VE BEEN GOING OUT FOR OVER A YEAR NOW.

(SNIFF) SO?

WE'RE IN HIGH SCHOOL. WE'RE SUPPOSED TO BE HONING OUR SOCIAL SKILLS IN PREPARATION FOR ADULTHOOD.

SO?

SO IF YOU AND I DON'T GET A CHANCE TO DATE OTHER PEOPLE, OUR INTERPERSONAL SKILLS ARE GOING TO BE SEVERELY UNDERDEVELOPED.

SO?

SO WE'RE NOT GOING TO KNOW HOW TO DEAL WITH THE OPPOSITE SEX, FOR STARTERS.

SO?

IT'S SOME CUTE LITTLE BLONDE, ISN'T IT.

DENISE, THERE ISN'T ANYONE ELSE — I JUST THINK WE NEED ROOM TO GROW.

GUYS ALWAYS DUMP THEIR GIRLFRIENDS FOR CUTE LITTLE BLONDES. WHO IS SHE?

THERE'S NO "OTHER WOMAN," OK?!

JUST LIKE A MAN — SOME CUTE LITTLE BLONDE COMES ALONG AND VROOM — IT'S OFF TO THE RACES!

DENISE, I DON'T WANT SOME CUTE LITTLE BLONDE!

APPARENTLY NOT.

THAT'S NOT WHAT I MEAN...

IN CASE ANYONE CARES, DENISE AND I BROKE UP. BUT I'M FINE AND I DON'T WANT ANYONE'S STUPID SYMPATHY.

I'M OLD ENOUGH TO HANDLE THIS ON MY OWN, THANK YOU. THE LAST THING I NEED IS MY FAMILY TO MAKE SOME HUGE DEAL OUT OF THIS!

JUST BECAUSE THIS IS THE MOST PAINFUL THING I'VE EVER GONE THROUGH, DON'T THINK FOR A MINUTE I NEED ANYONE TO—... PETER?

AMEND

...TALK TO.

I KNOW. C'MON—LET'S SIT DOWN.

I DON'T KNOW. I MEAN, DON'T YOU THINK IT'S BAD FOR SOMEONE TO JUST DATE ONE PERSON THROUGH HIGH SCHOOL?

WHY'S IT BAD?

WELL, I MEAN, DON'T YOU THINK THEY'LL END UP LIKE UNDERDEVELOPED SOCIALLY? LIKE THEY WON'T KNOW WHAT IT'S LIKE TO GO OUT WITH LOTS OF DIFFERENT GIRLS?

AMEND

THEY WON'T KNOW WHAT IT'S LIKE TO GO ON MILLIONS OF DATES, WONDERING IF THAT NEXT DATE IS GOING TO TURN OUT TO BE THAT SPECIAL SOMEONE.

INSTEAD, THEY'LL JUST BE STUCK WITH HER.

I HOPE YOU'RE LISTENING TO YOUR-SELF.

SO WHAT DO YOU THINK?

IT'S MORE IMPORTANT WHAT YOU THINK.

MOM, C'MON.

PERSONALLY, I THINK IF YOU FIND SOMEONE YOU REALLY CARE ABOUT, YOU SHOULD CONSIDER YOURSELF LUCKY. YOU SHOULD BE LOOKING FOR WAYS TO STRENGTHEN AND ENJOY THE RELATIONSHIP, NOT EXCUSES TO TEAR IT APART.

BUT WHAT ABOUT DATING?! HOW AM I GONNA LEARN ABOUT DATING?

PETER, DATING IS SIMPLY A MEANS TO AN END. YOU DATE TO FIND SOMEONE YOU CAN LOVE. WHY WOULD YOU LEAVE SOMEONE YOU LOVE SO YOU CAN DATE?

YOU'RE NOT MAKING THIS EASY FOR ME.

BREAKING UP SHOULDN'T BE.

AMEND

17

WOW—A "BATMAN" WALL CALENDAR! THANKS, SANTA!

JASON, WHAT DO YOU THINK YOU'RE DOING?

OPENING PRESENTS.

DON'T YOU THINK IT'S JUST A LITTLE EARLY TO BE OPENING PRESENTS?

IT'S CHRISTMAS MORNING. YOU'RE **SUPPOSED** TO GET UP EARLY ON CHRISTMAS MORNING.

IT'S 12:15 A.M., SON.

AMEND

12:17. SANTA GAVE ME A WATCH. WANNA SEE?

JASON, **PLEASE**...

I HAVEN'T FIGURED OUT HOW TO SET THE DATE YET...

JASON, PLEASE. IT'S THE MIDDLE OF THE NIGHT.

C'MON—I'VE ONLY GOT TWO PRESENTS LEFT TO UNWRAP, THEN I'LL GO BACK TO BED.

OK. FINE. TWO PRESENTS.

AMEND

TWO PRESENTS?!? THAT'S ALL YOU HAVE LEFT?!?

「OH,」 ROGER.

FINE, DAD—RUB IT IN.

WHAT'S WITH ALL THE MESS?

JASON OPENED ALL HIS PRESENTS AT MIDNIGHT.

I THOUGHT YOU TOLD HIM TO GO BACK TO SLEEP.

I WAS TOO LATE.

HE IS **SUCH** A LOSER.

PAIGE, LOOK—HE'S YOUNG. IT'S CHRISTMAS. IF THERE'S ONE DAY A YEAR WHEN WE OUGHT TO LET KIDS REALLY ENJOY THEMSELVES, IT'S CHRISTMAS. I DON'T LIKE WHAT HE DID, BUT IF IT MAKES HIM HAPPY...

AMEND

WOW—A FOOTBALL! THANKS, PAIGE!

RIP! RIP! RIP!

MOM—IT'S BEAUTIFUL! THANK YOU!

U.S.S. ENTERPR

27

WHAT DO YOU THINK?

IT LOOKS LIKE A PUDDLE OF BROWN PAINT.

IT'S ABSTRACT ART. I FIGURE IT'S GOOD FOR A WOMAN OF SUBSTANCE TO OCCASIONALLY EXPRESS HERSELF NON-VERBALLY.

PAIGE, IT'S A PUDDLE OF BROWN PAINT.

IT IS NOT. IT'S ART. IT EVOKES A MOOD. A FEELING. SEE HOW I'VE SWIRLED THE RED PAINT INTO THE GREEN PAINT? DON'T YOU **FEEL** IT?!

NAUSEA?

NO, SORROW! IT'S SUPPOSED TO BE **SAD**!

IT'S **VERY** SAD, PAIGE.

AMEND

WHAT'S THIS? "MONTY PYTHON"?

"MASTERPIECE THEATRE."

ICK! SINCE WHEN DID **YOU** START WATCHING BORING GROWN-UP SHOWS?!

MAYBE I'VE GROWN **UP**. MAYBE I'M NO LONGER CONTENT TO WATCH THE MINDLESS DRIVEL YOU **CHILDREN** FIND SO ENGAGING.

AMEND

IT'S A NEW DECADE. I'M A NEW PERSON. YOU'RE LOOKING AT THE PAIGE FOX OF THE '90s: A WOMAN OF SUBSTANCE, OF INTELLECT, OF DEPTH. YOU'RE LOOKING AT A WOMAN ON THE VERGE OF GREATNESS.

YOU'RE LOOKING AT A BOY ON THE VERGE OF THROWING UP.

LOOK, DON'T YOU HAVE **TOYS** TO PLAY WITH OR SOMETHING?

MOM, THIS NEW DECADE'S RESOLUTION ISN'T WORKING OUT THE WAY I THOUGHT IT WOULD.

OH?

I TRIED TO READ A MILLION BOOKS AND I COULDN'T GET THROUGH ONE. I TRIED TO PAINT AND ALL I GOT WAS A BROWN PUDDLE. JASON SAID I MAKE HIM WANT TO THROW UP AND I COULDN'T PUNCH HIS LIGHTS OUT.

I CAN'T KEEP THIS UP. I WANT TO BE ME AGAIN.

GOOD. I'M GLAD.

♪ OH, JASON DEAR... ♫

SORT OF.

AMEND

by Bill Amend

PAT PAT PAT PAT

LET'S SEE AN ICE AGE KILL OFF **THIS** DINOSAUR!

(SIGH) IF ONLY YOU WERE REAL.

AMEND

YOU'D LET ME RIDE ON YOUR BACK. WE'D GO EVERYWHERE TOGETHER.

YOU'D INTRODUCE ME TO ALL YOUR DINOSAUR FRIENDS. YOU'D TEACH ME TO SPEAK THE SECRET DINOSAUR LANGUAGE.

GROWL. GROWL.

NO ONE WOULD PICK ON US, 'CAUSE IF THEY DID, YOU'D EAT THEM.

YOU'D BE MY BEST FRIEND.

(SIGH)

Shake well before using.

FoxTrot
by Bill Amend

SQRPLTZZS

SHFITT
SHFITT
SHFITT

PAIGE?

AAAAAA!

HOW DO I THINK **UP** THESE THINGS?

WHY DO YOU THINK UP THESE THINGS?!

IT'S SUPER BOWL MONDAY.

SUPER BOWL MONDAY...

WHICH IS FOLLOWED BY SUPER BOWL TUESDAY.

SUPER BOWL TUESDAY...

THEN IT'S SUPER BOWL WEDNESDAY... SUPER BOWL THURSDAY... SUPER BOWL FRIDAY... SUPER BOWL SATURDAY... AND WE ALL KNOW WHAT COMES NEXT...

COMES NEXT...

AMEND

MOM GETS COMMITTED.

MOM GETS COM- ANDY, PLEASE!

WHOA—MY SKIN'S TINGLING ALREADY...

FIVE MORE DAYS! IF I CAN JUST MAKE IT THROUGH FIVE MORE DAYS!

ROGER, CALM DOWN.

SPORTS

AMEND

CALM DOWN?! WITH THE SUPER BOWL LESS THAN A WEEK AWAY?! THE NFC MEETING THE AFC IN A HEAD-TO-HEAD SHOWDOWN FOR THE NFL CHAMPIONSHIP?! YOU EXPECT ME TO CALM DOWN?!

MY GOD—FEEL MY HEART! IT'S GOING "HUT ONE, HUT TWO, HUT THREE,'" I'VE GOT TO GO TELL PETER!

FIVE MORE DAYS! IF I CAN JUST MAKE IT THROUGH FIVE MORE DAYS!

MOM, CALM DOWN.

ROGER, WILL YOU GO TALK TO YOUR SON.

WHAT'D HE DO NOW?

SPORTS DIGEST

HE WON'T DO HIS HOMEWORK. HE'S WATCHING SOME SUPER BOWL SPECIAL ON TV.

WHAT?!

I'VE SENT HIM TO HIS ROOM TWICE, BUT HE KEEPS SNEAKING BACK OUT TO WATCH. HE SAID IT WAS "REQUIRED VIEWING."

WHAT?!

AMEND

COULD YOU GO TALK SOME SENSE INTO—...

WHAT CHANNEL?

NOW WHAT ARE YOU MAKING?

YOU KNOW HOW EVERY OTHER CAR IN AMERICA HAS THOSE STUPID SUCTION-CUP GARFIELDS IN THE WINDOW?

YEAH...

I FIGURED IT WAS TIME TO CASH IN ON THE TREND. PRESENTING "JASON FOX'S AMAZING SUCTION-CUP LEECHES."

LEECHES?!

I'M GONNA BE RICH.

I'M GONNA BE SICK.

HERE, WATCH— STICK OUT YOUR HAND.

JASON, NO ONE IS GOING TO PAY MONEY FOR A SUCTION-CUP LEECH.

ARE YOU KIDDING? THESE BABIES ARE GONNA SELL LIKE HOTCAKES!

JASON, WHY WOULD ANYONE WANT A STUPID FAKE LEECH STUCK TO THEIR WINDSHIELD?!

AH, YOU SEE, THE BEAUTY OF THESE GUYS IS YOU CAN STICK THEM ANYWHERE.

REFRIGERATORS.. MIRRORS... WINDOWS... CEILINGS... FURNITURE... SISTERS...

AAAAA! YOU DIDN'T STICK ONE ON ME, DID YOU?!

THEY'RE GONNA SELL LIKE HOTCAKES.

WHAT'S THIS?

A SUCTION-CUP LEECH. WANNA BUY ONE?

WHAT ON EARTH WOULD I DO WITH A SUCTION-CUP LEECH?

STICK 'EM PLACES. THE GAG POTENTIAL IS LIMITLESS. WATCH— YOU JUST LICK 'EM AND...

AAAGH! ID'S STUG DO MA TUG! AAAGH!

I'M GAGGING ALL RIGHT.

SO... CAN I PUT YOU DOWN FOR A DOZEN?

WANNA COME SEE MY SUCTION-CUP LEECH SALES DISPLAY-UNIT PROTOTYPE?

No.

I MADE IT OUT OF A BUNCH OF CARDBOARD I FOUND IN THE GARAGE. DON'T YOU WANT TO COME SEE IT?

No!

NOW, IMAGINE IT WITH RED PAINT...

JASON, PLEASE...

AMEND

WHAT'S IN THE BAG?

WELL, AS YOU KNOW, I'VE BEEN TRYING TO SELL MY SUCTION-CUP LEECHES AT SCHOOL.

YES...

AFTER TWO DAYS OF FLAT SALES, I ASKED MYSELF, WHAT AM I DOING WRONG?

AND THEN IT HIT ME. WHAT THIS SALES CAMPAIGN NEEDS IS THAT CERTAIN JE NE SAIS QUOI.

AMEND

JE CERTAINLY NE SAIS QUOI.

NOW, THE JINGLE'S STILL A LITTLE RUSTY...

SO HOW GOES THE LEECH BUSINESS?

LOUSY. NOBODY AT HOME WANTS ONE... NOBODY AT SCHOOL WANTS ONE...

MAYBE AMERICA'S JUST NOT READY FOR SUCTION-CUP LEECHES.

MAYBE AMERICA'S JUST PLAIN STUPID.

AMEND

SO WHAT ARE YOU GOING TO DO WITH THEM ALL?

I GAVE 'EM TO PAIGE.

PAIGE WANTED THEM?!

NOT TO MY KNOWLEDGE.

AAAA!

by Bill Amend

FoxTrot

PETER AND JASON HAVE NEVER HAD COOKIES THIS GOOD.

...AND THEY'RE NOT GOING TO.

MMMM. CHOCOLATE CHIP COOKIES.

GET AWAY FROM THOSE! I'M BAKING THEM FOR **MY** CONSUMPTION!

I DIDN'T KNOW YOU KNEW HOW TO BAKE COOKIES.

THERE ARE A LOT OF THINGS ABOUT ME YOU DON'T KNOW.

HA!

YOU DON'T KNOW MY DREAMS... YOU DON'T KNOW MY ASPIRATIONS... YOU DON'T KNOW MY WISHES...

YOU DON'T KNOW MY THOUGHTS... YOU DON'T KNOW MY HOPES... YOU DON'T KNOW MY PRAYERS...

AMEND

YOU DON'T KNOW MY FEARS... YOU DON'T KNOW MY LONGINGS... YOU DON'T KNOW MY FRUSTRATIONS...

I KNOW THAT YOU AND NICOLE DIDN'T **REALLY** GO TO THE MOVIES FRIDAY NIGHT...

MMMM. CHOCOLATE CHIP COOKIES.

HELP YOURSELF.

Panel 1: SO HAS ANYONE ASKED YOU TO THE VALENTINE'S DANCE YET? / NO. I'M HOPING WILL CONRAD WILL ASK ME.

Panel 2: HE'S IN OUR BIOLOGY CLASS, RIGHT? / YEAH. I **KNOW** HE LIKES ME. I JUST WISH HE WEREN'T SO **SHY**. IT'S DRIVING ME NUTS.

Panel 3: I MEAN, IT'S NOT LIKE IT'S THE MOST DIFFICULT THING IN THE WORLD TO ASK SOMEONE TO A STUPID DANCE. WHAT'S HE SO AFRAID OF? WHAT'S THE WORST THING THAT CAN HAPPEN TO HIM?

Panel 4: YOU'LL SAY "NO," HE'LL BE SCARRED FOR LIFE, NEVER EVER DATE AND DIE OLD, LONELY AND UNLOVED. / **I'D** SAY I'M WORTH THAT RISK... / AMEND

Panel 5: HI, WILL. WHAT HAPPENED TO YOUR LAB PARTNER? / I DUNNO. I GUESS HE'S SICK OR SOMETHING.

Panel 6: WHAT A COINCIDENCE— **MY** PARTNER'S SICK, TOO. / REALLY? WOW.

Panel 7: HEY, I HAVE AN IDEA— WHY DON'T YOU AND I DO THIS LAB TOGETHER, SEEING AS HOW WE'RE BOTH PARTNERLESS? I MEAN, IF IT'S OK WITH YOU... / GOSH. YEAH. SURE. / AMEND

Panel 8: TEN BUCKS TO CUT CLASS— I CAN LIVE WITH THAT. / TEN?! SHE ONLY GAVE **ME** FIVE!

Panel 9: SO, WILL, HAVE YOU ASKED ANYONE TO THE VALENTINE'S DANCE YET? / ME? ARE YOU KIDDING?

Panel 10: WHAT DO YOU MEAN? / WHAT GIRL WOULD WANT TO GO TO A BIG-DEAL DANCE LIKE **THAT** WITH A GUY LIKE ME?

Panel 11: LOTS OF GIRLS. PLENTY OF GIRLS. TONS OF GIRLS.

Panel 12: ONE GIRL. / I THINK I WOULD'VE NOTICED BY NOW... / AMEND

45

AAAA! QUINCY—YOU CHEWED UP MY SWEATER!

BAD IGUANA! BAD, BAD, BAD IGUANA! BAD, BAD, BAD, BAD, BAD, BAD IGUANA!

WAIT A MINUTE— THIS IS PAIGE'S SWEATER.

SEMI-BAD IGUANA...

I THINK THIS WAS PAIGE'S FAVORITE SWEATER, TOO. YOU REALLY DID A JOB ON IT.

DANG. I GUESS THERE'S REALLY ONLY ONE THING WE CAN DO AT THIS POINT.

IT'S GONNA BE HARD, BUT SOMETIMES YOU JUST HAVE TO BOW YOUR HEAD, GRIT YOUR TEETH AND ADMIT THESE THINGS.

YOU WANT TO LEARN HOW TO KNIT?

GEEZ—DO YOU HAVE TO YELL IT?!

THERE. GOOD AS NEW.

GOOD AS ALMOST-NEW...

GOOD AS SORTA-ALMOST-NEW...

GOOD AS KINDA-WELL-WORN-AND-SLIGHTLY-FRAYED-SORTA-ALMOST-NEW...

WE'RE AS GOOD AS DEAD.

JASON, HAVE YOU SEEN MY PINK SWEATER?

PINK SWEATER?

MY RALPH LAUREN. THE ONE WITH THE LITTLE POLO PLAYER ON IT. I CAN'T FIND IT ANYWHERE.

NOPE. NO LITTLE POLO PLAYER SWEATERS IN HERE.

AMEND

CRUD.

YOU MUST'VE SWALLOWED THAT PART.

AAAA!
WHAT DID YOU DO TO MY SWEATER?!

QUINCY KINDA CHEWED ON IT.

LOOK AT IT— IT'S RUINED! THIS WAS MY FAVORITE SWEATER!

I KNOW. I'M REALLY SORRY. I TRIED TO FIX IT, BUT IT CAME OUT FUNNY. I FEEL AWFUL.

LOOK, JASON, DON'T FEEL BAD...

WHY NOT?

'CAUSE THEN I CAN'T PUNCH YOUR STUPID LIGHTS OUT!

DID I SAY "AWFUL"? I MEANT "SUPER AWFUL." ..."SUPER-DUPER AWFUL"...

JASON TOLD ME WHAT HAPPENED. HE FEELS TERRIBLE, YOU KNOW.

SNIFF.

I KNOW.

LISTEN—HE AND I HAVE WORKED OUT A LITTLE ARRANGE-MENT. HE'S BUYING YOU A NEW SWEATER.

THE EXACT SAME KIND?

THE EXACT SAME KIND.

AMEND

I HOPE...

HMMPH.

NOW, IT COST A LITTLE MORE, BUT...

SPIDERMAN

48

FoxTrot by Bill Amend

LET'S SEE...DO I WANT HEAT-SEEKING MISSILES OR A NUCLEAR-POWERED X-RAY LASER?

DESIGNING A HOUSE CAN BE SO CONFUSING.

WHAT **ARE** YOU DOING?

DRAWING UP BLUE-PRINTS FOR THE MANSION I'M GOING TO BUILD SOMEDAY. I'M CALLING IT JASON MANOR.

OF COURSE.

I FIGURE I'LL SAVE TIME BY PLANNING IT OUT NOW.

THIS IS THE MOAT WHICH SURROUNDS THE MAIN HOUSE. TO GET PAST IT, YOU HAVE TO USE THIS DRAWBRIDGE, WHICH CAN ONLY BE LOWERED BY AN EXACT MATCH OF MY VOICEPRINT. ANYONE BUT ME GETS PUSHED INTO THE MOAT BY THIS ELECTRIC ARM.

AMEND

THIS IS THE FRONT HALL. ANYONE BUT ME FALLS THROUGH A TRAPDOOR AND SLIDES DOWN A CHUTE INTO THE MOAT. THIS IS THE STAIRCASE. FOR ANYONE BUT ME, IT TURNS INTO A RAMP AND SENDS THEM TUMBLING OUT THE FRONT DOOR AND INTO THE MOAT.

THIS IS THE TV ROOM. ALL THE CHAIRS ARE TUNED TO MY EXACT WEIGHT. ANYONE BUT ME IS EJECTED THROUGH THE SKYLIGHT, OVER THE HOUSE, AND INTO THE MOAT. THIS IS THE KITCHEN—...

JASON, THIS IS RIDICULOUS! WHAT IF, FOR INSTANCE, I COME OVER TO VISIT?

WHOOPS—I HADN'T THOUGHT OF THAT...

TONING DOWN THE BOOBY TRAPS?

PUTTING SHARKS IN THE MOAT.

A NEW COMPUTER? WE CAN'T AFFORD A NEW COMPUTER.

THE NEWSPAPER'S GOING TO PAY FOR HALF OF IT. THIS WAY I CAN FILE MY COLUMN VIA MODEM.

BUT WE ALREADY **HAVE** A COMPUTER.

IT'S OLD, ROGER. THE NEWER ONES WILL LET YOU DO SO MUCH MORE.

SO WHAT KIND ARE YOU THINKING OF GETTING?

I'M NOT SURE. I SAW A COMMERCIAL FOR "THE COMPUTER FOR THE REST OF US."

THAT'S WHAT WE NEED, ALL RIGHT.

IT WAS UNCANNY.

PHOTON TORPEDOES LOCKED, SIR.

NOW, ARE YOU INTERESTED IN A COLOR OR A BLACK-AND-WHITE DISPLAY?

I PROBABLY JUST WANT BLACK-AND-WHITE.

WHOA.

I MUST POINT OUT THAT COLOR **DOES** HAVE ITS ADVANTAGES.

LOOK AT THIS, MOM—THE KLINGON SHIP IS METALLIC GREEN! I MEAN, **METALLIC GREEN!**

WHOA!—WHEN YOU TURN ON THE DEFLECTOR SHIELDS, THE SHIP KINDA HAS THIS PURPLE SHIMMER TO IT! LOOK AT THIS—YOU CAN SEE LITTLE ORANGE FLAMES COMING OUT OF THE ENTERPRISE! I SWEAR, I COULD PLAY THIS ALL DAY!

ZAP! ZAP! ZAP!

CLICK CLICK CLICK

...AND DISADVANTAGES.

I **DEFINITELY** JUST WANT BLACK-AND-WHITE.

WOW! DIDJA SEE THAT SUCKER **EXPLODE?!**

NOW, ANY QUESTIONS ABOUT THIS MACHINE?

CAN IT DO WORD PROCESSING?

YES.

CAN I HOOK A MODEM UP TO IT?

YES.

CAN MY SON PLAY HIS OLD APPLE II STAR TREK GAMES ON IT?

I'M AFRAID NOT.

I'LL TAKE IT.

MAN—THIS IS ONE COLD HOUSE.

TELL ME ABOUT IT.

WELL, LET'S SEE... IT'S GOT TWO STORIES, IT'S WHITE WITH GREEN TRIM, IT'S GOT FOUR BEDROOMS...

I'M FREEZING.

I'M FREEZING-ER.

OH? WELL, I'M FREEZING-ER-ER.

HA—I'M FREEZING-ER-ER-ER.

BIG WHOOP—I'M FREEZING-ER-ER-ER-ER.

SO? I'M FREEZING-ER-ER-ER-ER.

LOSER. I'M FREEZING-ER-ER-ER-ER-ER!

THAT'S NOTHING, ZIT-LIPS—I'M FREEZING-ER-ER-ER-ER-ER-ER!

LOSER! ZIT-LIPS!

AHEM.

ER...

ER-ER.

SO WHAT POSITION WILL YOU TRY OUT FOR THIS YEAR?

WELL, I THOUGHT OF PLAYING THIRD...

THE OL' HOT CORNER, EH? YOU KNOW, **I** PLAYED THIRD FOR A COUPLE YEARS. "SCOOPS" FOX, THEY CALLED ME. I REMEMBER THIS ONE GAME—BENNY "BATMAN" DEMOTT HIT A SHOT DOWN THE LINE—...

THEN I THOUGHT OF PLAYING SECOND...

THE PIVOT SPOT? I SPENT MY SOPHOMORE YEAR AT SECOND BASE! OL' "WILD BILL" KENNICK AND I HAD A DOUBLE-PLAY MOVE YOU WOULD NOT BELIEVE. ONE TIME—...

FINALLY, THOUGH, I SETTLED ON OUTFIELD.

HMMM... I'M NOT SURE I EVER PLAYED OUTFIELD...

I KNOW— I MEAN, OH, REALLY?

C'MON—THROW THE BALL.

DAD, YOU KNOW, IT'S GETTING AWFULLY DARK OUT.

PETER, I'VE HIT **HOME RUNS** IN LESS LIGHT THAN THIS!

C'MON—THROW THE BALL.

I ALREADY DID.

YOU KNOW, IT'S GETTING AWFULLY DARK OUT...

I'LL GO GET YOUR HAT.

SO HOW WAS YOUR LITTLE EXERCISE IN "FATHER-SON BONDING"?

IT WAS INCREDIBLE, ANDY, SIMPLY INCREDIBLE.

I MEAN, THE LOOK ON PETER'S FACE WHEN WE WERE DONE PLAYING CATCH...

I'VE NEVER SEEN HIM LOOK AT ME THAT WAY. IT WAS A LOOK OF CARING. A LOOK OF LOVE. A LOOK THAT SAID, "TALK TO ME, DAD."

ROGER, HE THOUGHT YOU WERE DEAD.

REGARDLESS. HMM —MUST'VE BEEN GRASS ON THE BALL...

54

FoxTrot by Bill Amend

HEE HEE HEE...

WHAT'S SO FUNNY?

THIS COMIC STRIP. IT REMINDS ME OF YOU.

WHAT?—THE ONE WITH THE "BOOGER BEING"?!

NO—THIS ONE. THE ONE WHERE THE KID PUTS A DEAD FISH IN HIS SISTER'S UNDERWEAR DRAWER.

WHAT'S THAT HAVE TO DO WITH ME?

OH, WAIT— YOU HAVEN'T GOTTEN DRESSED YET.

AMEND

MOTHERRRRRR!

HEE HEE HEE...

WHAT'S SO FUNNY?

AHEM.

HA! – TAKE **THAT,** KLINGON SCUM.

ZAP ZAP ZAP

JASON, I NEED TO USE MY COMPUTER.

LEMME JUST FINISH THIS GAME.

ZAP ZAP

JASON, I'VE GOT A COLUMN TO WRITE. HOW LONG'S THAT GOING TO TAKE?

HARD TO SAY. COULD BE MINUTES... COULD BE HOURS... COULD BE DAYS...

ZAP ZAP ZAP

COULD BE SECONDS... WHERE'S THE PLUG?

MOM, C'MON – I'M TRYING TO SAVE THE UNIVERSE!

ZAP ZAP ZAP

JASON, **PLEASE** – I'VE GOT TO WRITE MY COLUMN.

MOM, C'MON – I'M IN THE MIDDLE OF A GAME.

ZAP ZAP ZAP

CAN'T YOU JUST SAVE THE GAME AND FINISH IT LATER?

NO – THIS GAME DOESN'T LET YOU DO THAT.

BEEP

KLINGON WARSHIP APPROACH-ING

IT'S BASICALLY ONE OF THOSE GAMES THAT DOESN'T END UNTIL YOU BLOW UP.

ZAP BEEP ZAP

DO YOU REALLY **WANT** ME TO?

LET ME REPHRASE THAT: I MEAN, UNTIL I GET KILLED HMMM... LET ME REPHRASE **THAT...**

ZAP ZAP ZAP

THANK YOU.

I HOPE YOU FEEL GOOD ABOUT YOURSELF.

JASON, I BOUGHT THIS COMPUTER FOR **WORK,** REMEMBER?

I WAS ON A RECORD-SETTING PACE! ALL I HAD TO DO WAS KILL ANOTHER 126 KLINGONS AND I WOULD'VE MADE ADMIRAL!

BUT **NO** – BECAUSE OF **YOU,** I'M STUCK BEING A LOWLY CAPTAIN!

AND BECAUSE OF **YOU,** MY COLUMN'S GONNA BE LATE. NOW SHOO.

SHE WOULDN'T SAY "SHOO" TO AN ADMIRAL.

WHAT'S WITH YOU?

MOM.

WHAT'D SHE DO NOW?

SHE SCREWED UP THE GREATEST ACHIEVEMENT OF MY LIFE! SHE SQUASHED MY HOPES, DREAMS AND ASPIRATIONS! SHE PLUCKED ME FROM THE DAWN OF GLORY AND LEFT ME FEELING LIKE A COMPLETE LOSER!

SHE INTERRUPTED MY STAR TREK GAME ON THE COMPUTER.

WHAT'S WITH YOU?

PETER.

AMEND

JASON, WE NEED TO TALK.

HMMPH.

PETER TELLS ME YOU'RE STILL UPSET THAT I INTERRUPTED YOUR COMPUTER GAME.

MOM, I WAS **THIS CLOSE** TO SETTING A NEW RECORD! I WAS **THIS CLOSE** TO BECOMING A STAR FLEET ADMIRAL!

JASON, I **HAD** TO WRITE MY COLUMN. REAL LIFE HAS TO COME BEFORE GAMES.

STAR TREK **IS** MY LIFE.

JASON, WE **REALLY** NEED TO TALK.

OF COURSE, IT'D BE MORE FUN IF I WERE ALLOWED TO **LIVE** IT...

AMEND

JASON, I'M SORRY I INTERRUPTED YOUR GAME, BUT MY COLUMN WAS DUE. YOU **KNOW** THAT MY COLUMN HAS TO COME FIRST.

IT'S NOT FAIR — **MY** STUFF **NEVER** COMES FIRST.

THAT'S NOT TRUE.

IT **IS** TRUE. YOU AND DAD AND PETER AND PAIGE COULDN'T CARE LESS ABOUT THE STUFF THAT INTERESTS ME.

JASON, HONEY, YOU'RE **WRONG**.

PROVE IT.

AAAA! GO TO WARP SPEED!

NINETY-NINE PERCENT WRONG...

AMEND

57

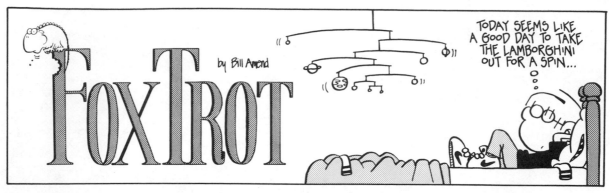

ROGER, DO YOU THINK YOU'LL EVER HAVE A NEED TO USE MY NEW COMPUTER?

POSSIBLY. WHY?

I HAVE SOME FREE TIME. I THOUGHT I COULD SHOW YOU HOW TO USE IT.

CAN'T IT WAIT?

AMEND

LET'S JUST SAY THE WARRANTY RUNS OUT NEXT WEEK.

I GET IT—YOU NEED OL' ROGER FOX TO PUT THE MACHINE THROUGH ITS PACES. YOU KNOW, TO SPOT PROBLEMS NOW BEFORE IT'S TOO LATE.

Marla Recants "Best Ever"

EXACTLY.

HMMM. WHAT'S IT MEAN BY "HARD DISK DESTROYED"?

OK, I'VE SET YOU UP WITH THE TUTORIAL DISK.

WILL IT DO SPREADSHEETS?

ROGER, YOU HAVE TO LEARN THE BASICS BEFORE YOU CAN DO ANYTHING FANCY.

ANDY, C'MON— THIS SORT OF STUFF IS INTUITIVE FOR ME. NOW HOW DO I MAKE IT DO SPREADSHEETS?

CLICK
CLICK
CLICK
CLICK
CLICK
CLICK
CLICK
CLICK
CLICK

OK, I'VE SET YOU UP WITH THE BACK-UP TUTORIAL DISK...

WILL IT DO SPREADSHEETS?

AMEND

JUST POINT AND CLICK.

POINT AND CLICK?

POINT AND CLICK.

POINT AND CLICK.

AMEND

CLICK

...AND TAKE TWO ASPIRIN.

WHERE'D ALL THE FILES GO?

ROGER, THIS WAS THE SIMPLEST COMPUTER THEY SOLD! **HOW** CAN YOU BE HAVING SO MUCH DIFFICULTY?!

WHO SAID I'M HAVING DIFFICULTY?

CLICK CLICK CLICK.

YOU'VE DESTROYED FOUR DISKS, ERASED HALF OF MY FILES AND CRASHED EVERY PROGRAM YOU'VE TRIED TO RUN!

ANDY, THOSE THINGS ARE BOUND TO HAPPEN NOW AND THEN.

NOW AND **THEN**?! ROGER, YOU'VE BEEN ON THE COMPUTER FOR ALL OF 15 MINUTES!

HEY—**YOU'RE** THE ONE WHO WANTED ME TO DO THIS. DON'T TELL ME **YOU'VE** NEVER MADE A MISTAKE.

CLICK CLICK CLICK

I MADE **ONE**...

DANG. WHAT DO THESE DISKS COST, ANYWAY?

COUGH

OK, I'VE GOT IT. WATCH.

CLICK

BLOOP. HARD DISK DESTROYED.

HMMM. WELL I **HAD** IT.

I'VE HAD IT.

OK, OK— **NOW** I'VE GOT IT...

SO HOW DID DAD'S LESSON ON THE COMPUTER GO?

DON'T KNOW YET. HE'S STILL AT IT.

BLOOOOOOP~

AAARGH!

AMEND

NEVER, NEVER, **EVER** AGAIN DO I WANT TO GET ANYWHERE **NEAR** THAT MACHINE!

STUPID COMPUTER.

I GUESS IT WAS A FAILURE.

I WOULDN'T SAY THAT...

OK, HERE YOU GO—1,000 SHEETS OF PAPER, TWO DOZEN BALLPOINT PENS AND THREE PLAIN BLUE BINDERS.

THANK YOU.

ENJOY.

I WILL.

I BETTER.

AMEND

MOM SAYS YOU'RE PLANNING TO WRITE A 900-PAGE ESSAY.

YUP. KINDA LEAVES YOU SPEECHLESS, DOESN'T IT?

IF I WERE WRITING 10 PAGES, YOU'D SAY "WOW." 25 PAGES WOULD ELICIT A "WHOA." BUT 900 PAGES JUST LEAVES YOU GRAPPLING FOR A SUITABLE WORD.

AMEND

900 PAGES. IT SIMPLY DEFIES DESCRIPTION.

NERD.

HMMM. MAYBE I OUGHT TO UP IT TO A THOUSAND.

I FIGURED OUT WHAT I'M GOING TO WRITE MY ESSAY ON.

OH?

IT'S GOING TO BE A RUNNING FIRST-PERSON ACCOUNT OF WHAT GOES INTO WRITING A 900-PAGE ESSAY.

I ALREADY HAVE MY FIRST SENTENCE FIGURED OUT. WANNA HEAR?

I'M AFRAID TO ASK...

AMEND

"THIS IS MY FIRST SENTENCE." WANNA HEAR THE SECOND SENTENCE?

I'M REALLY AFRAID TO ASK...

SO WHAT DO YOU THINK OF MY ESSAY SO FAR?

"...THIS IS MY FIFTH SENTENCE. THIS IS MY SIXTH SENTENCE. THIS IS MY SECOND PARAGRAPH..."

PRETTY GOOD, HUH?

GOOD?!

GREAT?

GREAT?!

INCREDIBLE?

BINGO.

MOM — I NEED HELP. MY ESSAY'S DUE TOMORROW.

HELP?!

PLEASE?

JASON, THIS HAPPENS EVERY TIME! YOU HATCH THESE HUGE, ELABORATE SCHEMES ONLY TO DISCOVER TOO LATE THAT YOU'RE IN WAY OVER YOUR HEAD AND NEED MY HELP.

JASON, I TOLD YOU A 900-PAGE ESSAY WOULD BE IMPOSSIBLE! I TOLD YOU YOU'D NEVER BE ABLE TO FINISH IT! WHAT MORE DO YOU WANT ME TO DO?!

PROOFREAD IT.

HELP.

DAD, I'M GONNA NEED HELP WITH MY ESSAY.

YOU'VE CERTAINLY COME TO THE RIGHT PERSON.

ESSAY-MAN FOX, THEY USED TO CALL ME. THERE WASN'T A BOOK I COULDN'T WAX POETIC ON, A SUBJECT I COULDN'T DISSECT WITH ELOQUENCE AND INSIGHT, A WORD I COULDN'T USE IN JUST THE RIGHT PLACE.

NOW HOW CAN I HELP?

OOF.

JUST PUT IT IN THE BACKSEAT.

69

by Bill Amend

FoxTrot

Theodore has a problem. He wants to eat exactly 12.5 percent of his apple at recess, 62.5 percent at lunch and the remaining 25 percent after school...

THEODORE'S GOT A PROBLEM, ALL RIGHT...

I HATE MATH.

PERSONALLY, I FIND IT RATHER ENRICHING. WHAT'S WRONG?

I CAN'T DO THIS ONE STUPID PROBLEM.

MAYBE I CAN HELP. READ IT TO ME.

"MARY LOU GOES SHOPPING. SHE BRINGS $50 WITH HER. SHE BUYS A $40 BLOUSE AT 30 PERCENT OFF, A PAIR OF SOCKS FOR 1/4 OF WHAT SHE PAID FOR THE BLOUSE, AN ICE CREAM CONE FOR 1/7 OF WHAT SHE PAID FOR THE SOCKS AND A SILK SCARF FOR HALF OF WHAT SHE HAS LEFTOVER."

"HOW MUCH MONEY DOES MARY LOU NOW HAVE?"

HMMM...

WELL?

THREE DOLLARS.

THAT'S THE ANSWER?

THAT'S MY FEE.

I REALLY HATE MATH.

AS I WAS SAYING...

AMEND

I REALLY WISH THE KIDS DIDN'T HAVE THE WHOLE WEEK OFF FROM SCHOOL.

WE'LL LIVE.

I REALLY WISH THEY'D AT LEAST FIND ANOTHER HOUSE TO TEAR APART.

WE'LL GET THROUGH THIS.

I REALLY WISH THEY COULD GO FIVE MINUTES WITHOUT FIGHTING.

WE'LL SURVIVE.

SPORTS

CARTOONIST TO TAKE MOUND OPENING DAY "Damn Right I'm Scared," Says Flustered Will Clark

I REALLY WISH YOU'D STOP SAYING "WE."

WHOA— I'M LATE FOR WORK.

AMEND

WHATCHA WATCHING?

"MATLOCK." IT'S A GOOD ONE. THERE ARE LIKE 25 SUSPECTS.

HAVEN'T YOU SEEN THIS ONE ALREADY?

NO.

AMEND

SURE YOU HAVE. IT'S THE ONE WHERE THE GIRL KILLS HER BROTHER.

I WALKED RIGHT INTO **THAT** ONE...

SUCH AN OBVIOUS MOTIVE. I'M DISAPPOINTED.

IT'S AMAZING HOW MUCH SPRING VACATION CHANGES WHEN YOU GET OLDER.

FOR NOW, IT MEANS JUST SITTING AROUND PLAYING VIDEO GAMES AND WATCHING "BULLWINKLE" RE-RUNS ALL DAY.

BUT IN ANOTHER 10 YEARS, IT'LL MEAN CHUGGING BEERS ON THE BEACH WHILE ENDLESS PARADES OF WOMEN COMPETE IN WET T-SHIRT CONTESTS.

AMEND

BETTER ENJOY IT WHILE WE CAN.

PASS THE HO-HOs.

THE GAME IS TIED... PETER FOX HAS THE BALL... THREE SECONDS LEFT... TWO... ONE...

HE SHOOTS!...

BUT WAIT—HE WAS FOULED! THE CROWD IS GOING NUTS!

HE MISSES.

THE CROWD?

THE GAME IS TIED... PETER FOX HAS 55 CHANCES TO MAKE A FREE-THROW...

OOO—THIS ONE CAME OUT WELL, DON'T YOU THINK?

JASON, YOU'VE COLORED ALL SEVEN OF YOUR EGGS GREEN!

EIGHT.

WHATEVER. IT'S WEIRD!

AMEND

I FIGURE THIS WAY WHEN THE EASTER BUNNY HIDES THEM OUTSIDE, WE WON'T BE ABLE TO FIND THEM ALL. PRETTY SOON THEY'LL ROT, THE YARD WILL BE CRAWLING WITH RATS AND YOU'LL WANT TO MOVE OUT.

A LITTLE LATE FOR ST. PATRICK'S DAY, AREN'T WE?

IS THERE **NO** ONE IN THIS HOUSE WITH A SENSE OF HUMOR?!

SPORTS ILLUSTRATED

KIDS, HURRY UP! WE'RE GOING TO BE LATE FOR CHURCH!

HOW DO I LOOK?

WHY, PAIGE, YOU LOOK LOVELY!

THANK YOU.

I JUST LOVE EASTER. I LOVE CHRISTMAS, TOO, BUT WITH EASTER, EVERYBODY ALWAYS DRESSES UP EXTRA SPECIAL. EXTRA SPRINGY. EXTRA PRETTY. EXTRA EASTERY.

AMEND

EXTRA WEIRD.

I DON'T LOOK WEIRD, DO I?!

DO YOU EVER.

by Bill Amend

FoxTrot

MUNGLRP SKMFD GLGRM

PFTHSK CHMPF MNGRLG

SO WHAT'S MOM MAKING FOR BREAKFAST?

WHAT DO YOU THINK YOU'RE DOING?

NOT NOW, MOM... GRGLMN CHOMPG YMNLGH

MPLMN GLRGF YUGLNM

TIME OUT! WHAT IS GOING ON?

WE'RE HAVING A RACE TO SEE WHO CAN EAT THEIR CHOCOLATE RABBIT THE FASTEST.

MGRGP GLMK CHOGMP

THAT'S A POUND OF CHOCOLATE! YOU'LL MAKE YOURSELVES SICK!

HEY, JASON—SHE SAID TIME-OUT! MOM, C'MON, WE'RE KIDS.

FINE. YOU CAN HAVE A PENALTY BITE.

WHAT'S THAT HAVE TO DO WITH IT? **PAIGE** IS A KID— I DON'T SEE HER GOBBLING DOWN **HER** RABBIT!

OF COURSE YOU DON'T.

AND WHY DO YOU THINK **THAT** IS?...

BECAUSE SHE'S FINISHED. WE'RE BATTLING FOR SECOND.

BETTER HURRY UP, PAL—I'M ALMOST DONE WITH THE EARS.

AMEND

I JUST DID SOMETHING THAT I MAY REGRET FOR THE REST OF MY LIFE.

WHAT?

LET'S JUST SAY I'VE SUNK TO A NEW LOW. I DON'T KNOW IF I CAN LIVE WITH MYSELF.

WHAT'D YOU DO?

I MEAN, I **KNEW** IT WAS A MISTAKE, IT'S JUST THAT THE PRESSURE KINDA CLOUDED MY JUDGMENT. WHAT WAS I **THINKING**?!

PAIGE, WHAT DID YOU **DO**?!

I ASKED JASON TO TUTOR ME IN MATH.

WHY, LOOK— ANOTHER GRAY HAIR.

"THE BRAIN" IS READY TO SEE YOU NOW.

AMEND

OK. WHAT YOU NEED TO DO HERE IS SUBSTITUTE X FOR Y+3.

JASON, WILL YOU TAKE OFF THAT STUPID BRAIN HAT?!

LOOK, **YOU'RE** THE ONE WHO WANTED ME TO HELP YOU STUDY.

I WANTED HELP WITH MATH, NOT SOME "NERDS ON PARADE" COSTUME SHOW!

AMEND

FINE. BUT I'M NOT AS SMART WITHOUT MY EXTERNAL BRAIN.

I DON'T CARE. TAKE IT OFF.

DID I SAY Y+3? I MEANT Y+6,000,000.

YOU SCREW ME UP AND YOUR BRAINS'LL BE EXTERNAL, ALL RIGHT.

WHAT'D YOU GET FOR PROBLEM SIX?

$2\sqrt{x}$.

$2\sqrt{x}$?! YOU GOT $2\sqrt{x}$?!

HOW ON **EARTH** DID YOU GET $2\sqrt{x}$?! I CAN'T **BELIEVE** YOU GOT $2\sqrt{x}$!

IT'S WRONG?

AMEND

NO, IT'S **RIGHT**. I'M SHOCKED.

OH, WAIT— DID YOU SAY PROBLEM **SIX**?...

HEY, PAIGE—IF THE KITCHEN'S IN THE HOUSE, AND DIANA'S IN THE KITCHEN, WHAT'S IN DIANA?

I DUNNO. WHAT?

A STATE.

WHAT??

IN-DIANA. GET IT?

PETER, THAT'S THE STUPIDEST JOKE I'VE EVER HEARD.

A STATE.

WHAT??

ALL RIGHT! A GLOW-IN-THE-DARK BRACHIOSAURUS!

YAHOO.

BET YOU'RE JEALOUS.

OH, YEAH. RIGHT.

BET YOU'RE DYING WITH ENVY. BET YOU'RE CRYING INSIDE. BET YOU'RE FURIOUS THAT I GOT TO IT BEFORE YOU DID. ADMIT IT—IT BUGS YOU.

JASON, IT DOESN'T BUG ME, OK?!

DID I MENTION THAT IT GLOWWWS IN THE DAAARK?

NOW YOU, ON THE OTHER HAND...

PETER?

UH...(AHEM) ...YEAH.

YOU DON'T SOUND LIKE PETER.

UH...(AHEM) I...ER... STRAINED MY VOICE YELLING AT JASON.

MMM. WELL, THEN, WHY DON'T YOU SIT HERE AND CUDDLE WITH ME A WHILE AND MAYBE YOU'LL FEEL BETTER.

CUDDLE?! WHAT DO YOU MEAN, "CUDDLE"?! BLECH!

ACTUALLY, YOU DO SOUND A LITTLE LIKE PETER.

OF COURSE I DO. WHAT'S WITH JASON?

FoxTrot
by Bill Amend

TOMORROW'S THE FIRST DAY OF MAY.

YEAHHH...

THE DAY AFTER THAT IS THE SECOND DAY OF MAY. THE DAY AFTER THAT IS THE THIRD DAY OF MAY.

AMEND

AND THE DAY AFTER **THAT** IS...

THE FOURTH. BIG WHOOP.

FOR SOME OF US IT IS.

OH, WAIT—THE A'S PLAY THE RED SOX. OK.

IT'S MY BIRTHDAY, YOU MORON!

FRIDAY?

YES. I CAN'T BELIEVE YOU FORGOT.

I DIDN'T **FORGET**. HOW STUPID DO YOU THINK I AM?

YOU DIDN'T **SAY** ANYTHING. YOU CERTAINLY **ACTED** LIKE YOU DIDN'T KNOW.

IF I ACTED LIKE I **REMEMBERED** YOU WOULDN'T BE **SURPRISED**.

AMEND

ACTUALLY, I'D BE **VERY** SURPRISED.

I MEAN, DO YOU **REALLY** THINK I'D FORGET AGAIN AFTER **LAST** YEAR?

PAIGE, IF YOU WERE DENISE, WHAT WOULD YOU WANT FOR YOUR BIRTHDAY?

HMMM. AM I MAD AT YOU?

A LITTLE. YEAH.

DIAMONDS. BIG OL' ROCKS.

WHAT IF YOU WEREN'T MAD AT ME?

HMMMM...

NEVER MIND.

DIAMONDS. BIG OL' ROCKS.

AMEND

ROGER, DARLING, YOU AND THE KIDS WOULDN'T HAPPEN TO BE, OH, PLANNING ANYTHING SPECIAL FOR MOTHER'S DAY, WOULD YOU?

NO, WHY?

I MEAN, OF COURSE NOT! WHY DO YOU ASK?

Cartoonist Pitches 5th No-Hitter— Ruining Game, says frustrated Gwynn

APPARENTLY BECAUSE I HAVE TO.

(PSST. HEY, KIDS...)

AMEND

SHHH. OK, KIDS, LISTEN UP— THIS SUNDAY IS MOTHER'S DAY, SO WE NEED TO FIGURE OUT WHAT TO GET YOUR MOM.

ANY SUGGESTIONS?

GET HER FLOWERS.

GET HER ROSES.

GET HER A LIFE-SIZE INFLATABLE ALLOSAURUS.

AMEND

GET SOME CANDY. DEFINITELY.

GET THE GOOD KIND.

GET SOME HELIUM, TOO. THAT WAY IT'LL FLOAT.

JASON, GET REAL.

GET A LIFE.

GET AWAY FROM ME.

GET A COUPLE. YOU KNOW, IN CASE ONE LEAKS.

WHATCHA DOING?

MAKING A SHOPPING LIST. I'M COOKING DINNER FOR MOTHER'S DAY.

AMEND

I THINK I'VE GOT EVERYTHING COVERED— FRENCH BREAD... SALAD STUFF... BONELESS CHICKEN BREASTS...

...BATTERIES.

BATTERIES?

FOR THE SMOKE ALARM. I FIGURE YOU'LL DRAIN THE ONES WE'VE GOT. YUK YUK YUK.

HA HA. VERY FUNNY. I ALWAYS TAKE 'EM OUT BEFORE I START.

HMMPH.

JASON, WHY THE GLUM FACE?

PAIGE IS COOKING DINNER FOR MOTHER'S DAY, PETER'S BUYING MOM FLOWERS AND YOU'RE GETTING HER CANDY.

SO?

SO WHAT'S LEFT FOR ME TO GIVE HER?

YOU COULD CLEAN YOUR ROOM...

HENCE THE GLUM FACE.

MAYBE YOU COULD JUST CLEAN THE REST OF THE HOUSE INSTEAD— I'M SURE SHE'D UNDERSTAND.

AMEND

FLOWERS? PETER, THANK YOU!

YOU COOKED DINNER? PAIGE, THANK YOU!

YOU CLEANED YOUR ROOM? JASON...

...THANK YOU THANK YOU THANK YOU KISS KISS KISS THANK YOU THANK YOU THANK YOU KISS KISS KISS...

SHOW-OFF.

I GUESS I KNOW WHO TO GIVE THE EXTRA-BURNT CHICKEN TO.

AMEND

WELL, IT'S BEEN AN INTERESTING MOTHER'S DAY.

WHAT DO YOU MEAN BY "INTERESTING"?

WELL, LET'S SEE... JASON STUFFED THE ENTIRE CONTENTS OF HIS ROOM INTO PAIGE'S CLOSET, PETER SPILLED A WATER-FILLED VASE ALL OVER THE KITCHEN AND TRIED TO MOP IT UP WITH KLEENEX AND PAIGE NEARLY SET HER HAIR ON FIRE COOKING A DINNER THAT NO ONE ATE.

AMEND

IT STRUCK ME THAT IF I WEREN'T AROUND, THIS PLACE WOULD COLLAPSE IN A DAY OR TWO.

IT'S A NICE FEELING. SORT OF.

CHOCOLATE DOESN'T STAIN, DOES IT?

by Bill Amend

WAAA HA HA HA HA
HA HA HA HA HA HA
HA HA HA HA HA HA HA
HA HA   HA HA
HEE
HEE HEE   GIGGLE
HEE   GIGGLE
HEE HEE   GIGGLE
          (SNIFF)

DANG, I'M FUNNY.

WHAT ARE YOU DOING?

DRAWING A COMIC STRIP.

WHAT FOR?

DOES EVERYTHING HAVE TO HAVE A **REASON**? CAN'T SOMEONE CREATE SOMETHING SIMPLY FOR THE SHEER JOY OF IT?

EXCUSE **ME**, MR. PHILOSOPHER.

HAVEN'T YOU EVER HEARD OF SELF-EXPRESSION? HAVEN'T YOU EVER HEARD OF ART FOR ART'S SAKE?

AMEND

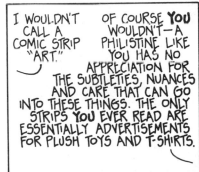

I WOULDN'T CALL A COMIC STRIP "ART."

OF COURSE **YOU** WOULDN'T—A PHILISTINE LIKE YOU HAS NO APPRECIATION FOR THE SUBTLETIES, NUANCES AND CARE THAT CAN GO INTO THESE THINGS. THE ONLY STRIPS **YOU** EVER READ ARE ESSENTIALLY ADVERTISEMENTS FOR PLUSH TOYS AND T-SHIRTS.

I, ON THE OTHER HAND, RECOGNIZE THE LIMITLESS POTENTIAL OF THE ART FORM AND SIT HERE NOW SAVORING **NOT** THE ANTICIPATION OF A HUGE LICENSING DEAL, BUT RATHER THE BEAUTIFUL AND CHALLENGING ACT OF CREATION.

AND IT **IS** BEAUTIFUL.

"BARF AND ARF"?!

EVEN THE TITLE IS POETRY.

Panel 1: Slug-Man stares helplessly as the pendulum of doom swings ever closer...

Panel 2: It's going to take the best mind in the business to get out of this one. Fortunately, he's got it. The blade is now only inches from his chest. Time is running out. He's got to think of something. Fast!

Panel 3: Could this be the end of Slug-Man?! Will Slug-Man survive?!

Panel 4: MISS GRINCHLEY— JASON'S DRAWING ON HIS DESK.

WILL SLUG-MAN'S **CREATOR** SURVIVE?...

Panel 5: JASON, MISS GRINCHLEY TELLS ME YOU WERE DRAWING CARTOONS ON YOUR DESK.

YES, SIR.

Panel 6: WOULD YOU CARE TO EXPLAIN?

WELL, IT STARTED OUT SMALL—JUST A COUPLE OF LITTLE DOODLES THAT I DIDN'T THINK ANYONE WOULD NOTICE.

Panel 7: THE NEXT THING I KNEW, IT HAD MUSHROOMED INTO THIS EPIC MASTERPIECE. EACH DAY I WOULD ADD A LITTLE SOMETHING TO IT. I CALL IT "SLUG-MAN BATTLES MISS GRINCHLEY."

Panel 8: HARDLY A FAIR FIGHT.

WELL, I GAVE MISS GRINCHLEY TENTACLES.

Panel 9: MOM? IT'S ME, JASON.

JASON? WHAT'S WRONG?

Panel 10: MR. RAWTHROAT WANTED ME TO LET YOU KNOW THAT I HAVE TO STAY AFTER SCHOOL.

WHAT'D YOU DO?

Panel 11: I KINDA DREW A FULL-SCALE SLUG-MAN ADVENTURE ON MY DESK. IN PERMANENT INK.

GREAT.

Panel 12: LARRY HERE WILL SHOW YOU WHERE THE "409" IS KEPT.

SEE YOU MONDAY.

WHADJA DRAW ON YOUR DESK FOR, ANYWAY?

I DUNNO. EVERY TIME I DRAW SLUG-MAN ON PAPER, MY IGUANA EATS IT.

I GUESS SUBCONSCIOUSLY I WANTED TO GIVE SLUG-MAN SOME PERMANENCE. I WAS SICK AND TIRED OF HAVING MY DRAWINGS CHEWED UP INTO LITTLE SPITBALLS. I WANTED THIS COMIC BOOK TO LAST.

AMEND

THAT'S PROBABLY WHY I USED INDELIBLE INK.

OBVIOUSLY YOU HAVEN'T MET LIL' BETSY HERE.

CAN I JUST READ IT ONE MORE TIME?

CAN'T YOU DO IT?

KID, C'MON— MR. RAWTHROAT SAID THAT YOU HAD TO CLEAN THE DESK.

I CAN'T! I CAN'T WIPE AWAY A WEEK'S WORK LIKE THIS! THIS WAS THE BEST SLUG-MAN ADVENTURE YET! LOOK AT THOSE EXPRESSIONS! LOOK AT THE FORCED PERSPECTIVE ON THE SLUGMOBILE!

I'M SORRY, KID, BUT THERE'S NOTHING YOU CAN DO ABOUT IT.

AMEND

NOW WAIT JUST A MINUTE...

KID, YOU EXPLAIN IT...

ART PRESERVATION LADY. WE'RE GONNA NEED SOME BIG PAPER.

XEROX 5250

ARE YOU MAD AT ME?

OF COURSE I AM. JASON, WHAT YOU DID WAS WRONG AND YOU KNOW IT.

I'M SORRY.

MARKING UP YOUR DESK AT SCHOOL IS AS MUCH AN ACT OF VANDALISM AS SPRAY-PAINTING YOUR NAME ON THE WALL!

AMEND

LOOK, I ALREADY GOT THIS LECTURE FROM MR. RAWTHROAT.

OK, OK. BUT PROMISE ME THE NEXT TIME YOU WANT TO DRAW SLUG-MAN CARTOONS YOU'LL DO IT ON PAPER. MAYBE THE REST OF US WOULD LIKE A CHANCE TO SEE WHAT YOU'RE DRAWING.

I XEROXED MY DESK.

I SAID "MAYBE."

OK, SCHOOL, THIS IS IT — I'VE HIT ROCK BOTTOM.

I WILL SAY YES TO ANYONE WHO ASKS ME TO THE PROM. ANY TAKERS?...

I THOUGHT I'D HIT ROCK BOTTOM...

WHY, LOOK AT ME — ALL DRESSED UP AND WITH A PLACE TO GO.

EAT SPIT AND DIE.

IS POOR WIDDLE PAIGY-WAIGY UPSET?? JUST BECAUSE SHE'S NOT GOING TO THE PROMMMM?

RING RING RING

MOTH-ERRR!

PETER — TELEPHONE.

LIFE CAN BE SO UNFAIR.

DENISE — YOU CAN'T BE SICK!

AND THEN AGAIN...

DENISE IS SICK?!

SHE'S GOT THE CHICKEN POX! CAN YOU BELIEVE IT?! TWO HOURS BEFORE THE PROM!

POOR DENISE.

POOR DENISE?! WHAT ABOUT POOR PETER?! I SPENT $60 RENTING THIS TUX... $50 FOR MY SHARE OF THE LIMO... $40 ON TICKETS... ALL WASTED!

IT DOESN'T HAVE TO BE WASTED — YOU CAN STILL GO.

WHAT — BY MYSELF?!

TAKE PAIGE.

I SAID "POOR PETER," NOT "COMMITTABLY INSANE PETER."

PAIGE, DO YOU STILL WANT TO GO TO THE PROM?

MOTHER, THIS ISN'T SOMETHING TO KID ABOUT.

I'VE FOUND YOU A PROM DATE. DO YOU STILL WANT TO GO?

LOOK, EVERYONE'S KIDDED ME ABOUT THIS ENOUGH ALREADY.

HE'S NICE... HE'S INTELLIGENT... HE'S HANDSOME... HE'S AVAILABLE...

MOTHER, PLEASE! I KNOW YOU'RE KIDDING!

HE'S YOUR BROTHER...

I CERTAINLY HOPE YOU'RE KIDDING.

AMEND

OK. I'M READY.

I WANT YOU TO KNOW THAT THIS WAS ENTIRELY MOM'S IDEA.

I HAD ABSOLUTELY NOTHING TO DO WITH THIS. THIS IS HER DOING, NOT MINE. SHE IS RESPONSIBLE FOR THIS, NOT ME.

AMEND

GOT IT.

OK. LET'S GO.

HAVE FUN.

BE REALISTIC, MOTHER.

I EXPECT YOU TO THANK ME FOR THIS.

I CAN'T BELIEVE I'M AT THE PROM WITH MY SISTER.

I FEEL LIKE THE BIGGEST LOSER ON EARTH. LOOK AT US STANDING HERE LIKE TWO WORLD-CLASS GOOBERS ON DISPLAY.

NOTHING COULD BE WORSE THAN THIS. NOTHING COULD BE WORSE THAN STANDING AROUND ONE'S OWN PROM WITH ONE'S DWEEBY LITTLE SISTER FOR A DATE. NOTHING.

AMEND

LET'S DANCE.

EXCEPT...

HEE HEE HEE...

WHAT ARE YOU DOING?

PLANNING OUT THE HAUNTED HOUSE I'M GOING TO BUILD IN MY ROOM FOR HALLOWEEN.

THAT'S LIKE FIVE MONTHS AWAY!

THESE THINGS TAKE TIME. THE FLOATING ZOMBIES **ALONE**'LL TAKE ME A FEW WEEKS TO BUILD AND DEBUG.

FLOATING ZOMBIES. IN YOUR BEDROOM. IN JUNE.

I FIGURED I'D PUT 'EM IN THE CORNER NEXT TO THE WEREWOLF VICTIM DIORAMA. DANG, THIS IS GONNA BE SCARY!

GOING TO BE?!

AMEND

WHAT IS JASON **DOING?!**

HE'S BUILDING A HAUNTED HOUSE.

WHAM! WHAM! WHAM!

NO, SERIOUSLY, WHAT'S HE DOING?

HE'S BUILDING A HAUNTED HOUSE FOR HALLOWEEN.

IT'S **JUNE!**

HE WANTED TO GET A JUMP ON THINGS.

WHAT DO YOU THINK? IS THE FLESH GREEN ENOUGH?

SOMETHING MAY JUST JUMP ON **HIM.**

MAKE THAT SOME-THINGS.

AMEND

GO AWAY!

I'M DOING RESEARCH FOR MY HAUNTED HOUSE.

I DON'T CARE— GO AWAY!

HOW WOULD YOU DESCRIBE YOUR REACTION TO THIS SAMPLE SPECTRE: (A) SHOCK OR (B) TERROR?

(C) OTHER.

WHAT DO YOU MEAN, "(C) OTHER"?

AMEND

GO AWAY!

I'M DOING RESEARCH FOR MY HAUNTED HOUSE...

MOM, ARE YOU GOING TO THE GROCERY STORE ANY TIME SOON?

WHY?

AMEND

COULD YOU PICK UP SOME KETCHUP? I'LL NEED ABOUT 10 BOTTLES.

TEN BOTTLES?! WHAT ON EARTH FOR?

I'M TURNING MY ROOM INTO A HAUNTED HOUSE FOR HALLOWEEN AND I FIGURED I'D USE KETCHUP FOR BLOOD.

HALLOWEEN'S IN OCTOBER. THE KETCHUP'LL BE ALL DRIED-UP AND MOLDY BY THEN.

THAT'S THE IDEA. LET'S SEE... THERE WAS SOMETHING ELSE I NEEDED...

A TALKING TO?

JASON, WE NEED TO TALK.

WATCH WHERE YOU STEP.

RIP

ABOUT?

ABOUT THIS HAUNTED HOUSE BUSINESS. IT'S JUNE, HONEY. I CAN'T LET YOU GO AND TURN YOUR BEDROOM INTO SOME SORT OF CARNIVAL SHOW FIVE MONTHS BEFORE HALLOWEEN IT'S JUST NOT HEALTHY.

RIP

AMEND

BUT...

AAAA!

*SPROING!

I SAID WATCH WHERE YOU STEP...

IT'S NOT HEALTHY FOR ANY OF US.

RIP

HEY— YOUR ROOM'S BACK TO NORMAL!

YEAH. MOM MADE ME PUT MY HAUNTED HOUSE ON HOLD UNTIL HALLOWEEN.

WHAT'D YOU DO WITH EVERYTHING? THIS ROOM WAS FILLED WITH RUBBER ZOMBIES, SKELETONS AND SPIDERS A FEW HOURS AGO.

I PUT SOME IN THE CLOSET AND SOME UNDER THE BED.

AMEND

IN PAIGE'S ROOM, NO DOUBT.

CALL ME A FOOL FOR FUN...

CALL HIM AN AMBULANCE.

PAIGE, MOM SAYS YOU HAVE TO GET UP.

NNNGH.

PAIGE, C'MON — WAKE UP!

WILL YOU GET OUT OF HERE?! I'M TRYING TO SLEEP!

MOM SAYS YOU'VE SLEPT LONG ENOUGH.

FOR CRYING OUT LOUD — IT'S THE FIRST MONDAY OF SUMMER VACATION! WHAT'S THE BIG DEAL?!

THE FACT THAT IT'S TUESDAY?

GIMME FIVE MORE MINUTES...

AMEND

WHAT'S WITH THE ALL-BLACK LOOK?

I'M MOURNING THE END OF ANOTHER GLORIOUS SCHOOL YEAR.

NINE MONTHS OF TOTAL AND UNWAVERING SUCCESS. "A+" AFTER "A+." 100 PERCENT AFTER 100 PERCENT. ALL RELEGATED TO HISTORY NOW. ALL PUT TO REST IN THE LAND OF PAST TENSE. DO YOU HAVE ANY IDEA HOW DEPRESSING IT IS?

AMEND

BUT THEN, HOW COULD YOU?

WHAT'S WITH THE ALL-BLACK-AND-BLUE LOOK?

HA HA. I'VE ALREADY HEARD IT.

WELL, IT'S SUMMER VACATION.

YUP.

WHAT DO YOU WANT TO DO?

I DUNNO. I'VE PRACTICALLY FORGOTTEN WHAT ONE DOES ON VACATION.

AAAA! MOTHERRR — JASON'S STUPID IGUANA CHEWED UP MY NEW BLOUSE!

AMEND

VACATE.

AH, YES.

LOOK AT MY REPORT CARD, QUINCY— STRAIGHT "A"S!

ISN'T IT GREAT?! ISN'T IT TERRIFIC?! AREN'T YOU PROUD OF ME?!

OK, OK, SO I **COULD**'VE GOTTEN AN "A+" IN MATH, BUT **STILL**...

AMEND

PETER, WOULD YOU LIKE ME BETTER IF I WEREN'T BLIND?

LIKE YOU **BETTER**?!

DENISE, I LIKE YOU AS MUCH AS ANYONE CAN LIKE ANYONE AS IT IS!

YOU'RE WONDERFUL! YOU'RE PERFECT! YOU'RE THE BEST GIRLFRIEND EVER! I COULDN'T **POSSIBLY** LIKE YOU MORE THAN I ALREADY DO! WHAT KIND OF QUESTION **IS** THAT?!

AMEND

APPARENTLY, A PRETTY GOOD ONE.

"LIKE" ISN'T EVEN THE WORD I'D USE. WELL, MAYBE IT IS...

MOM, WHERE'S DAD'S MAGNIFYING GLASS?

WHAT DO YOU WANT IT FOR?

SOMETHING.

JASON, I DON'T WANT YOU FRYING ANTS, DO YOU HEAR ME?

AMEND

WHY ON EARTH WOULD I WANT TO FRY ANTS?! THEY'RE CUTE! THEY'RE INTELLIGENT! ANTS ARE OUR **FRIENDS**!

IT'S IN HIS DRESSER.

...UNLIKE CERTAIN SISTERS.

ZZZZ...

99

PAIGE, YOU KNOW HOW I'VE ALWAYS TAUGHT YOU TO KEEP YOUR WORD? YES...

HOW I'VE ALWAYS SAID YOU SHOULD NEVER BREAK A PROMISE? YES...

AMEND

HOW I'VE STRESSED THE IMPORTANCE OF COMMITMENT? MOM, WHAT ARE YOU GETTING AT?

ANDY, C'MON—TEE TIME'S IN A HALF-HOUR. SUPPOSE I WERE TO SET A REALLY BAD EXAMPLE... LOOK, I FEEL FOR YOU, BELIEVE ME...

ROGER, WE HAVE TO GO BACK. I FORGOT MY GOLF CLUBS. I PUT 'EM IN THE TRUNK.

I FORGOT MY GOLF SHOES. I GOT 'EM.

I FORGOT MY GOLF GLOVE. I PACKED IT.

I FORGOT MY SUNSCREEN. I THREW IT IN WITH MY STUFF.

HELP ME OUT. WHAT **DIDN'T** YOU PACK? HERE WE ARE— LUCKY DUFF'S LUCKY LINKS...

AMEND

ROGER, WHAT **ARE** YOU DOING?! CHECKING THE WIND.

HURRY UP. THERE ARE PEOPLE WAITING. ANDY, PLEASE— IT'S THE FIRST HOLE. THEY UNDERSTAND.

UNDER-STAND WHAT? THAT THE FIRST SHOT OF THE FIRST HOLE IS VERY IMPORTANT. IT CAN SET THE TONE FOR THE WHOLE DAY.

AMEND

HONEY, LET'S JUST GO HOME... THEY **DO** UNDER-STAND. OK, CLUB, THERE'S THE FLAG...

YOUR KNEES ARE TOO STIFF.

YOUR HEAD'S TOO HIGH.

YOUR GRIP'S ALL WRONG.

YOUR AIM IS OFF.

FORE...

OK, IT'S A STRAIGHT AND LEVEL THREE-FOOT PUTT. YOU CAN DO IT.

DON'T CHOKE.

WHAP

SORRY. COMPETITIVE REFLEX.

DO ME A FAVOR— DON'T MOVE.

MY GOD, THAT STUPID GAME TOOK AN ETERNITY.

IT SEEMED TOO SHORT TO ME.

AN ETERNITY OF WALKING OVER AN ENDLESS NUMBER OF HILLS. AN ETERNITY OF WHACKING AT AN ENDLESS STREAM OF BALLS. AN ETERNITY OF PUTTING, CHIPPING AND ARGUING.

BET YOU CAN'T WAIT FOR A REMATCH.

I HATE TO BEAT THE WORD "ETERNITY" TO DEATH, BUT...

HOW 'BOUT TOMOR-ROW?

PETER, THREE WEEKS AGO WE TALKED ABOUT YOU GETTING A SUMMER JOB.

TWO WEEKS AGO WE TALKED ABOUT YOU GETTING A SUMMER JOB.

LAST WEEK WE TALKED ABOUT YOU GETTING A SUMMER JOB.

WHAT ARE YOU **WAITING** FOR?!

SEPTEMBER?

AMEND

EVER WONDER HOW SUPER-MAN CAN FLY?

ALL THE TIME.

I THINK IT HAS SOME-THING TO DO WITH HIS MOLECULAR MAKE-UP.

I THINK IT HAS SOME-THING TO DO WITH THE GRAVITY ON KRYPTON.

MOTHERRR— JASON PUT DADDY-LONG-LEGS IN THE ICE-CUBE TRAY!

OR MAYBE IT'S SOMETHING SIMPLER...

COULD BE.

AMEND

JIM GERNAND CALLED LAST NIGHT.

JIM GERNAND?! **THE** JIM GERNAND?!

MM-HMM.

HE'S LIKE THE BIGGEST HUNK IN SCHOOL! PAIGE, I CAN'T BELIEVE HE CALLED! THAT'S **SO** COOL!

AMEND

WHAT'D HE SAY?? WHAT'D **YOU** SAY??

"PETER'S NOT HOME."

SO HE MIGHT CALL **BACK**?...

HEY, KIDS—GUESS WHO'S HAVING PIZZA FOR DINNER!

YOU GOT PEPPERONI, I HOPE.

YOU DIDN'T GO TO THAT GREASY PLACE YOU WENT TO LAST TIME, DID YOU?!

PLEASE TELL ME YOU DIDN'T GET MUSHROOMS.

GUESS WHO'S HAVING A **LOT** OF PIZZA FOR DINNER...

YOU DIDN'T GET ONIONS ON THEM, DID YOU?

AMEND

MOM, I NEED TO USE THE CAR.

WHERE ARE YOU GOING?

AMEND

OBVIOUSLY TO THE MALL.

DID SOMEONE SAY "MALL"?!

SHHHH!

WHAT A CUTE LITTLE BUTTERFLY.

YEAH. QUINCY LIKES 'EM THAT WAY.

QUINCY?

I GUESS THE BIGGER ONES TAKE TOO LONG TO CHEW.

BLECH! WHY DO YOU TELL ME THESE THINGS?!

AMEND

ISN'T IT OBVIOUS?

FoxTrot by Bill Amend

CLEAN MY ROOM?! MOTHER, ARE YOU KIDDING?!

NO.

JUST CHECKING.

MOTHER, LOOK WHAT I FOUND WHILE I WAS CLEANING MY CLOSET.

AWWW. IT'S YOUR OLD TEDDY BEAR. WHAT WAS IT YOU USED TO CALL HIM?

GRIZZLY-POOH. I CAN'T BELIEVE HE STAYED HIDDEN AWAY SO LONG.

YOU NEVER LET THAT BEAR OUT OF YOUR SIGHT WHEN YOU WERE LITTLE.

I REMEMBER WHEN JASON WAS A BABY, GRIZZLY-POOH USED TO SCARE HIM TO DEATH.

SO NATURALLY YOU WAVED GRIZZLY-POOH IN HIS FACE EVERY CHANCE YOU GOT.

NATU-RALLY.

HEE HEE. I WONDER IF JASON REMEMBERS ME DOING THAT.

PAIGE, **THINK** ABOUT IT.

HMM. I GUESS HE **WAS** PRETTY LITTLE...

QUINCY WANTS TO SEE YOUR ZIT.

AMEND

HEY—I WAS WATCHING "MURDER, SHE WROTE"!

TOUGH. "THE SIMPSONS" IS ON.

CLICK

THEY'RE ALL REPEATS.

SO?

SO YOU'VE PROBABLY SEEN THIS EPISODE HALF A DOZEN TIMES!

THE SUBTLETIES OF THE SHOW DEMAND REPEAT-ED VIEWINGS. YOU HAVE TO SEE EACH EPISODE AT LEAST 10 TIMES FOR YOUR BRAIN TO FULLY GRASP IT.

AMEND

OR FOR IT TO FULLY GRASP YOUR BRAIN.

DIDJA HEAR THEY'RE MAKING A BART SIMPSON TALKING TOOTHBRUSH?

JASON, I WANT TO WATCH "MURDER, SHE WROTE"!

DON'T HAVE A COW, MAN.

AND KNOCK OFF THAT STUPID BART SIMPSON TALK!

AY CARAMBA.

AMEND

I SAID KNOCK IT OFF!

AY CARAMBA AY CARAMBA AY CARAMBA AY—...

...SWOLLEN?

SAVE THE JOKES FOR MY LAWYER.

♪ AH... CAIN'T GET NOO-O... SATIS—... ♪

SHIKA SHIKA SHIKA

PFFFFFFFT

WHO USED UP ALL MY MOUSSE?!

AMEND

JASON, PLEASE...

"BART." OK, OK, SKIP THE WALLPAPER. JUST BUY ME ALL THE T-SHIRTS.

WHAT'S THIS?

IT'S A LIST OF ALL THE SIMPSON PRODUCTS.

WHY ARE YOU GIVING THIS TO ME?

I DUNNO. IN CASE YOU'RE EVER SHOPPING AND FEEL THE URGE TO WIN YOUR YOUNGEST CHILD'S EVERLASTING LOVE AND AFFECTION!

JASON, I WOULD HOPE THAT YOUR EVERLASTING LOVE AND AFFECTION DOESN'T HINGE ON MY BUYING YOU A SIMPSON PRODUCT.

GOOD LORD NO.

JUST CHECKING.

PRODUCTS. PLURAL.

AMEND

JASON, WE NEED TO TALK.

ABOUT?

ABOUT YOUR LITTLE OBSESSION WITH "THE SIMPSONS."

WHAT ABOUT IT?

It's bad enough that you've done God-knows-what to your hair. It's bad enough that you quote strange snippets of Bart-speak throughout the day. But what absolutely **MUST** stop is this incessant begging for Simpson paraphernalia.

I THOUGHT YOU AND DAD WOULD **WANT** TO MAKE ME HAPPY.

WE **WANT** TO BE ABLE TO PUT YOU THROUGH COLLEGE.

BUY ME THE CARPETING AND I WON'T ASK FOR ANOTHER THING — I SWEAR!

AMEND

WHAT HAPPENED TO THE "BART SIMPSON" LOOK?

I'VE BEEN TIPPED OFF THAT THE FAD IS PASSÉ.

AMEND

IT WAS "COOL" YESTERDAY AND IS "PASSÉ" TODAY??

THAT'S THE WAY IT GOES WITH FADS.

TOO BAD YOU DIDN'T TELL PAIGE THIS — SHE JUST BOUGHT A "SIMPSONS" T-SHIRT.

TELL PAIGE?

ABOUT THE TIP.

SHE **WAS** THE TIP.

COOL, HUH?!

Don't Have a Cow, Man!

by Bill Amend

AH ONE, TWO,
AH ONE, TWO, THREE, FOUR—

FIVE.

SINCE MA BABY
LEFF ME...

DA!

AH FOWNA NEW
PLACE TO DWELL...

DA!
DA!

DOWN AT THE ENDA
LONELY STREET, AT...

HEART-
BREAK
HOTEL...

YOU MEAN
"EARACHE
HOTEL."

I'D SAY
"HEADACHE
HOTEL."

"SHAMPOO-BOTTLE-STUFFED
DOWN-HIS-STUPID-THROAT
HOTEL!"

TOO MANY
SYLLABLES,
PAIGE.

AMEND

109

WHAT'S THE RUSH? IT'S ONLY QUARTER PAST.

MY SUMMER INTERN STARTS TODAY. I WANT TO GET SOME THINGS READY FOR HIM TO DO.

OH? HAVE YOU MET THIS PERSON?

NO. HE'S SOME KID FROM PEMBROOK'S ALMA MATER. IMPRESSIVE RESUMÉ.

I DUNNO. I'VE NEVER TRUSTED RESUMÉS.

ANDY, ANDY, ANDY — I SEE RESUMÉS ALL THE TIME. BELIEVE ME, THIS KID'S SOMETHING SPECIAL. HERE, TAKE A LOOK.

"CAREER OBJECTIVE: TO BE JUST LIKE ROGER FOX."

READ THE PART ABOUT HIS UPCOMING SENIOR THESIS...

MR. FOX? I'M SKIP RILEY. YOUR SUMMER INTERN?

OH, SKIP. NICE TO MEET YOU.

THE PLEASURE IS ALL MI —...

WHAT'S WRONG?

YOUR OFFICE. SOMEHOW I EXPECTED AN EXECUTIVE OF YOUR STATURE AND REPUTATION TO HAVE SOMETHING A LITTLE LARGER. YOU KNOW, PALATIAL.

WELL, THIS IS WHAT THEY GAVE ME.

MY GOD — BRILLIANT, DYNAMIC, FORCEFUL AND TOLERANT. SIR — TEACH ME. MOLD ME.

YOU'RE HERE 'TIL WHEN? SEPTEMBER?

ANDY, THIS KID IS INCREDIBLE.

WHAT KID?

MY NEW INTERN. HE TAKES DIRECTION... HE'S EAGER TO PLEASE... HE WANTS TO LEARN...

THAT'S GREAT.

HE'S PERFECT, ANDY! HE'S ABSOLUTELY PERFECT!

ROGER, NO ONE'S PERFECT.

SIR, I'VE DECIDED THAT YOU'RE PERFECT.

(ANDY, I'M TELLING YOU...)

YOU'RE HERE A LITTLE EARLY, AREN'T YOU?

ACTUALLY, I'VE BEEN HERE FOR TWO HOURS NOW.

TWO **HOURS**?!

YES, SIR. I WANTED TO GET A JUMP ON THINGS.

I DIDN'T REALIZE I'D GIVEN YOU THAT MUCH TO DO.

SIR, I'M OF THE OPINION THAT ONE SHOULDN'T WAIT FOR WORK TO BE GIVEN OUT. SOMETIMES YOU HAVE TO SEE A VOID AND FILL IT.

AMEND

...OR REPAINT IT.

I HOPE YOU LIKE THE COLOR.

YOU SHOULD **SEE** THIS KID, ANDY!

ROGER, WILL YOU QUIT BABBLING ABOUT THIS NEW INTERN?!

DAD?

I'M SORRY, BUT SINCE HE'S STARTED, I FEEL ENERGIZED. LIKE I'M **SOMEBODY**. I CAN'T HELP IT.

AMEND

DAD? WANNA PLAY CATCH?

I FEEL ALIVE. IMPORTANT. WISE. SPECIAL. **NEEDED**.

ROGER...

NOT TO MENTION DEAF.

HE PAINTED MY OFFICE, ANDY. HE PAINTED MY **OFFICE**!...

ROGER...

WHAT TIME DO YOU WANT TO GO TO THE DRIVING RANGE?

OH, PETER— I'M NOT GOING TO HAVE TIME FOR THAT TODAY.

BUT YOU **PROMISED**! I'VE BEEN PRACTICING MY SWING ALL WEEK!

I KNOW, BUT MY NEW INTERN SKIP SCORED A COUPLE OF TICKETS TO THE BALL GAME. WE CAN PLAY GOLF TOMORROW.

YOU UNDERSTAND, DON'T YOU?

ALL TOO WELL.

HEY, LISTEN— CAN SKIP BORROW YOUR HAT? IT'S PRETTY SUNNY OUT.

AMEND

by Bill Amend

FoxTrot

WHAT TO COOK...
WHAT TO COOK...

I CAN TELL YOU WHAT **NOT** TO COOK...

I'VE ONLY GOT TWO HOURS, DEAR.

WHAT'S FOR DINNER?

I WAS THINKING OF MAKING MEAT LOAF.

BLECH!

PAIGE, **PLEASE!** DO YOU HAVE ANY IDEA HOW COMPLICATED IT IS TO COOK FOR THIS FAMILY?

IF I MAKE FISH, SOMEONE COMPLAINS. IF I MAKE CHICKEN, SOMEONE COMPLAINS. NOW YOU AND JASON TELL ME YOU HATE MEAT LOAF.

JASON HATES MEAT LOAF?

HE CLAIMS IT MAKES HIM GAG.

DID I SAY "BLECH"? I MEANT "MMMM."

DID I SAY "COMPLICATED"?...

AMEND

PETER, COULD YOU PLEASE TAKE OUT THE GARBAGE?

WHY DON'T YOU ASK **HIM** TO DO IT?

WHO'S "HIM"?

YOUR STUPID INTERN. FOR THE PAST WEEK ALL YOU'VE DONE IS RAVE ABOUT HOW PERFECT HE IS. CALL HIM UP—I'M SURE HE'D **LOVE** TO DRIVE OVER AND TAKE OUT YOUR TRASH.

MAYBE I **SHOULD** INVITE HIM OVER. MAYBE YOU'D **LEARN** A FEW THINGS.

WHAT—LIKE HOW TO STEAL YOUR AFFECTION?!

PETER, I DON'T LIKE WHAT I'M HEARING.

THEN IGNORE ME. YOU'RE GETTING GOOD AT IT.

PETER, I'M SORRY YOU FEEL BAD—IT'S NOT MY INTENT...

I DON'T FEEL **BAD**, DAD—I FEEL INVISIBLE.

AMEND

I DON'T KNOW WHAT YOU MEAN.

ALL YOU DO ANYMORE IS TALK ABOUT THIS "SKIP" LIKE HE'S THE GREATEST KID ON EARTH. IT'S LIKE YOU DON'T EVEN KNOW I **EXIST**.

THAT'S NOT TRUE.

IT **IS** TRUE! I WANTED TO PLAY CATCH AND YOU DIDN'T EVEN NOTICE! WE WERE SUPPOSED TO GO TO THE DRIVING RANGE AND YOU WENT OUT WITH **HIM** INSTEAD! I FINISHED READING THAT KIPLING BOOK YOU GAVE ME AND YOU DIDN'T EVEN SAY A WORD!

I THOUGHT I GAVE THAT BOOK TO SKIP...

MR. FOX? I FINISHED PROOFING THE PRITCHARD DRAFT.

ALREADY?

WELL, SIR, YOUR WRITING IS SO CLEAR AND ERROR-FREE THAT PROOFING IT IS HARDLY WORK. IN FACT, I TOOK LONGER THAN I MIGHT HAVE SIMPLY BECAUSE I FOUND MYSELF SAVORING AND RE-READING YOUR ARTFUL WORDPLAY.

HEE HEE. SKIP, I THINK YOU'RE EXAGGERATING JUST A TAD.

SIR, I NEVER EXAGGERATE.

OH.

MAY I GO TO LUNCH NOW, MY LIGHT AND INSPIRATION?

MAY I JOIN YOU?

AMEND

Panel 1:
HELLO, FOX. WHO'S YOUR FRIEND?

SKIP RILEY. MY SUMMER INTERN.

Panel 2:
SKIP, THIS IS CHARLES DIGGS—HE HEADS OUR DEPARTMENT.

I KNOW. SIR, IT IS WITH PROFOUND PLEASURE THAT I NOW SIT IN YOUR GLORIOUS PRESENCE.

Panel 3:
HEE HEE. THAT'S NOTHING—YOU SHOULD HEAR WHAT HE SAYS ABOUT ME.

THANK YOU, SKIP.

YOU TRULY ARE MY LIGHT AND INSPIRATION.

Panel 4:
I AM⁇

NO NO— I AM.

VERILY. TAKE MY SEAT. PLEASE.

AMEND

Panel 5:
YOU'RE **WHAT**⁈

RESIGNING AS YOUR INTERN. MR. DIGGS WANTS ME IN **HIS** OFFICE.

Panel 6:
HE CAN'T **DO** THAT! **YOU** CAN'T DO THAT! I HAD YOU FIRST!

IT'S MY DECISION. AND I'VE MADE IT.

Panel 7:
WHY⁇ I THOUGHT YOU **LIKED** ME! I WAS YOUR "LIGHT AND INSPIRATION," YOUR "RAISON D'ÊTRE," YOUR "STANDARD OF PERFECTION"!...

YOU WERE, BUT NOW MR. DIGGS IS. I'M HERE TO GET A RECOMMENDATION FOR GRAD SCHOOL AND LET'S FACE IT—DIGGS IS A BIG CHEESE. YOU'D DO THE SAME THING IN MY SHOES.

AMEND

Panel 8:
NO, I DON'T THINK I WOULD.

WELL, I GUESS THAT'S WHY YOU'RE JUST A LEVEL-B MANAGER. TOODLES.

Panel 9:
HE JUST UP AND QUIT?

CHUCK DIGGS FELL FOR HIS ACT AND OFFERED HIM AN "EXECUTIVE" INTERNSHIP. CAN YOU BELIEVE IT?

Panel 10:
YES.

AS SOON AS DIGGS TOOK AN INTEREST IN HIM, I EFFECTIVELY CEASED TO EXIST. I DON'T UNDERSTAND IT.

AMEND

Panel 11:
HE PAID ATTENTION TO ME... HE WAS INTERESTED IN EVERYTHING I DID... HE WANTED TO **DO** THINGS WITH ME... I **THOUGHT** HE WAS MY **BUDDY**!...

Panel 12:
I KNOW THE FEELING.

PETER, I'M SORRY.

WHAT'S ALL THIS? JASON'S CHARGING UP THE CAMCORDER BATTERIES.

YOU BOUGHT A CAMCORDER?! NO NO NO— MARCUS' PARENTS ARE LENDING US THEIRS TO TAKE ON VACATION.

PHEW. SO WHERE IS IT? WHERE DO YOU THINK?

I SAID GET OUT! MUTUAL OF OMAHA PRESENTS...

WHAT ARE YOU DOING?! VIDEOTAPING YOUR EVERY MOVE.

Revlon! Cosmopolitan

WHY?? IN CASE YOU DO SOMETHING STUPID, LIKE WALK INTO A WALL, I WANT TO GET IT ON TAPE FOR THAT TV SHOW.

"AMERICA'S FUNNIEST HOME VIDEOS"? "FUNNIEST"? I THOUGHT IT WAS "UGLIEST."

Revlon! Cosmopolitan

GIMME THE CAMERA— I HEAR "RESCUE 911" NEEDS SOME FOOTAGE. YOU'RE SURE IT'S NOT "UGLIEST"?

(WE'VE SECRETLY REPLACED THE FINE COFFEE NORMALLY SERVED HERE WITH A JAR OF DIRT.)

(LET'S SEE IF ROGER FOX CAN TELL THE DIFFERENCE...)

CarToonist to Repair Hubble Telescope

SLUUURPRPRP...

SLUUURPRPRP... ...BEFORE I GET SICK.

ZZZZ...

PAIGE, WAKE UP! — YOU'RE COVERED WITH SPIDERS!

AAAA! GET 'EM OFF! GET 'EM OFF! GET 'EM OFF!

♪ SMILE. YOU'RE ON CANDID CAM—... ♪

I GUESS THERE'S A REASON WHY THEY HIDE THESE THINGS.

I'M GOING TO **KILL** THAT LITTLE TWERP!

WHAT'S HE DOING NOW?

HE'S FOLLOWING ME AROUND WITH THAT STUPID VIDEO CAMERA!

STILL? WASN'T HE DOING THAT ALL DAY YESTERDAY?

HE'S BEEN DOING IT ALL **WEEK**! HE'S WAITING FOR ME TO DO SOMETHING FUNNY SO HE CAN GET ON THAT DUMB TV SHOW.

MAYBE IF YOU IGNORE HIM...

OK, NOW WHEN YOU GO OUT BACK, PRETEND YOU DON'T SEE THE PIT, OR THE TRIP-WIRE.

I DON'T **DARE** IG-NORE HIM.

JASON, SOME-ONE'S LIABLE TO GET HURT...

PAIGE, C'MON DOWN — JASON'S GOING TO PLAY THE VIDEO HE SHOT OF YOU.

CLICK

JASON FOX PRESENTS... A JASON FOX PRODUCTION... OF A JASON FOX FILM...

"BIGFOOT: FACT OR FICTION?"

SCRATCH THAT.

WE BEGIN OUR SEARCH IN THE KITCHEN..

OK, LET'S SEE... IF HE EATS ALL HIS FOOD, I GIVE HIM A TUMMY RUB.

RIGHT.

AND IF HE STAYS QUIET ALL NIGHT, I GIVE HIM A MEALWORM.

RIGHT.

BUT IF HE SNEAKS OUT AND BUGS MY SISTERS...

AMEND

I GIVE HIM A TUMMY RUB **AND** A MEALWORM.

I'M GONNA MISS YOU, QUINCE.

THIS IS **IT**?

THAT'S IT.

YOU'RE SURE?

I'M SURE.

AMEND

NOTHING ELSE?

NOTHING ELSE.

FINALLY.

SORRY. ONE MORE.

WELL, DENISE, I GUESS THIS IS IT...

MMM...

I'LL MISS YOU...

ME TOO...

HECK, I'LL ONLY BE GONE TWO WEEKS...

I KNOW...

AMEND

SOON TO BE **ONE** WEEK.

WELL, DENISE, I GUESS THIS IS IT...

MMM...

WELL, I EXPLAINED TO THE KIDS THAT EVENTUALLY YOU'LL UNLOCK THE CAR.

GOOD.

I TOLD THEM THAT UNTIL THEN, THEY SHOULD JUST TRY TO HAVE FUN DESPITE YOUR ROYALLY SCREWING THINGS UP.

WHAT'D THEY SAY?

AMEND

"NO PROBLEM."

THOSE KIDS ARE REAL TROOPERS. OF COURSE, I'M NOT SURPRISED.

"...WE'RE USED TO IT."

WE SURE ARE. DANG—THE COATHANGER'S STUCK AGAIN.

BEANS?! THAT'S IT?!

WE HAVE HOT DOGS, BUT THEY'RE LOCKED IN THE CAR.

AMEND

DO WE AT LEAST HAVE SOME SODA?

THAT'S IN THE CAR, TOO.

THIS IS RIDICULOUS!

TELL IT TO YOUR FATHER.

DAD, THIS IS NO LONGER FUNNY.

LIKE IT'S SUPPOSED TO BE?!

BRRR—IT'S COLD.

YOU'RE PRETTY GUTSY PUTTING YOUR FOOT IN THE LAKE LIKE THAT.

WHY?

I THOUGHT YOU WITCHES MELTED UPON CONTACT WITH WATER.

AMEND

SHUT UP.

I GUESS YOUR NATURALLY GREASY SKIN KEEPS YOU SAFE.

BRRR—IT'S COLD.

YOU'RE PRETTY GUTSY FLYING HEADFIRST INTO THE LAKE LIKE THAT.

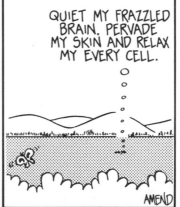

FoxTrot

by Bill Amend

OH, HI MARCUS. I DIDN'T HEAR YOU COME IN.

I'M PRACTICING MY NINJA STEALTH TECHNIQUE. IS JASON HOME?

HE'S UPSTAIRS.

HMMM. MIND IF I USE THE TRELLIS?

WAS QUINCY A GOOD BOY WHILE JASON WAS AWAY?

WELL, LET'S SEE...

HE CHEWED UP MY SISTER DOREEN'S RUNNING SHOES...

HE THREW UP MEALWORMS AND APPLE CHUNKS ON MY SISTER LISA'S PILLOW... HE SNUCK UNDER MY SISTER LANA'S SHEETS AT THREE IN THE MORNING...

AND HE DID SOMETHING IN MY SISTER CYBIL'S ROOM, BUT WE HAVEN'T YET FIGURED OUT EXACTLY WHAT.

HE REALLY DID ALL THAT?

YUP.

HE **WAS** A GOOD BOY...

GOOD NOTHING. **GREAT.**